Lessons from
Valley View

Lessons from Valley View

Caleb Clayton Sellers

Rural Renaissance
Publishing

Rural Renaissance Publishing
Bonifay, Florida

ISBN: 979-8-218-66563-0

First Edition, 2025

Cover and design by Caleb Clayton Sellers

Image Credit: *1969 Chevrolet Camaro SS* (p. 28-29). Original image sourced from a Chevrolet advertisement (1969). Courtesy of www.camaros.org. Used under fair use for commentary and illustrative purposes.

For permissions, inquiries, or information regarding bulk orders, signed copies, classroom use, bookstore partnerships, or author visits, please contact: calebclaytonsellers@gmail.com

To Pawpaw,
with love,
Pete

epigraph

Had our share of the pain
Of the clouds and the rain
Lean on me and I'll lean on you
And together, we'll get through
We always do

— Ray LaMontagne, "We'll Make It Through"

program

overture

Growing up in the rural South makes you familiar with the traditions of fishing, hunting, and sports— hobbies I associated with a masculinity I never seemed to possess. I never found killing innocent animals as something worth to be excited about, and the idea of sweating my ass off in the sun to plant some tomatoes never seemed enjoyable to me either. But my Pawpaw loved every bit of it, and he was determined to make us love it too.

My cousins and I were put through the wringer of digging trenches, just like our moms were when they were little. We all hated doing it, but we did it for him.

A seed of resentment for these customs made me reject it even more as a teenager. In joining art, band, and culinary, I found comfort in creative expression, something that I never found outside.

When I came out to my parents at sixteen, it may have been slightly rocky to our new beginning, but quickly in time, I was reassured that my parents loved me unconditionally and would always be proud of the child that made them parents. However, I never felt that acceptance from anyone else in my family, and it's not because they said anything. I just assumed, for all my childhood, that no one else in my family would see me the way my parents did.

This made me feel like I would never belong to the Rushings. I used to always think that because my cousin was the one that would enjoy hunting and fishing that Pawpaw favored him more. For so long, I had always felt a sense of silent rejection from my extended family, and it made me reject everything about my hometown and family in protest, leading me to find escape at Florida State.

I never officially came out to Pawpaw, so I never knew how he saw me. But in my later high school years, we bonded over my school success, my art, my music, and my writing. It was hard to love myself when I felt so different from the mold everyone else seemed to fit. But eventually, I realized there was a place for me all along. That gift of music, writing, and knowledge all came from Pawpaw just as much as his talents in fishing and hunting did. I quickly learned that what *we* shared in common were the gifts *I* excelled in and the hobbies *he* held close to his heart.

When I told him I was graduating with my associate's degree before even finishing high school, he looked at me and said, "I couldn't do that." Mawmaw and I glanced at each other in shock. *Bill (Cleve Earl) Rushing* had just admitted there was something he couldn't do—something *I*, Caleb Clayton Sellers, his gay grandson, had accomplished. I will never forget that day

prelude i

prologue

*it is better to be silent and be thought a fool, than to open
your mouth and remove all doubt*

lessons from
valley view

by caleb sellers

*dedicated
to the life of*
Cleve Earl Rushing

act i

I make enough mistakes
And it feels like he's the only one that hears the things I say
So if for any reason there's some miscommunication
Or I'm lying to your face
My immaturity and habits getting in the way
'Cause I can barely breathe
And I don't know how I'll explain myself this time
Wish it wasn't a case of this life
But why can't I be any other man
That doesn't need a hand in love
Someone that I could trust
But how would I fail
To give you all the love that you deserve
When he's the only thing that's worth what life is worth
And I don't mind if you hate me
'Cause, maybe, if I were you,
I would probably hate me too

—   *Lyrics adapted from "Untitled" by Rex Orange County*

As part of my African American Studies secondary major, I was required to complete an internship of my choice during my final semester at Florida State University.

Among the many opportunities that intrigued me, I chose to intern at 621 Gallery in the Railroad Square Art District. I had always loved drawing and painting in middle and high school, but once I began college, I gradually abandoned my creative hobbies. This internship felt like the perfect opportunity to rekindle my passion for art.

As an intern, I leaned into my English major by organizing and curating a monthly poetry reading event. I had never done anything like that before, so I lacked a lot of confidence. But being surrounded by other young creative minds lit a spark in me I never realized I needed. For the first time, I felt like I had found my people and my voice as an artist.

In the final month of my internship, an opening became available in the Nan Boynton Memorial Gallery. One of my fellow interns suggested that we all collaborate on an exhibition to showcase the talents of those working behind the scenes of 621 Gallery. We brought the idea to our director and president, and it was instantly approved.

Our exhibition was titled *Who We Are*, and it birthed my first—and slightly unpolished—project: a collection of sixteen poems that tell the story of my late grandfather who always said,

 "I want you to write a book about me."

This was an opportunity for me to create something that would be displayed for all of Tallahassee to see, so it only felt right to create an exhibition that fulfilled my Pawpaw's dream. I'm deeply grateful to 621 Gallery for making me feel like a real, respected artist and for always making me feel welcome when I return.

. . .

In the process of writing, editing, and designing this book, I discovered a newfound respect for the poems that confirmed what I already believed—my writing was a gift from God, passed down from my grandfather. Therefore, in honor of where this book began, I now invite you to visit its original form.

These are *Lessons from Valley View (2022)*.

This collage-style cover was born
from my love of digital collage art. At the time,
I envisioned *Lessons from Valley View* as a poetry zine.

it is better to be silent and be thought a fool, than to open
your mouth and remove all doubt

lessons from
valley view

by caleb sellers

dedicated
to the life of
Cleve Earl Rushing

Title page featuring a picture
of the Valley View Community Center
which once served as Cleve Earl's elementary school.

lessons from
valley view

by
caleb sellers

Dedicated to myself—an ode
to my sense of accomplishment, my healing through grief,
and the beginning of my writing career.

for me
in more ways than one

Chapter I – The Bright Light
originally titled to signify his birth

Cleve Earl's sophomore portrait c. 1958

"Prelude" originally served as the opening to the collection—like the introduction to a symphony.

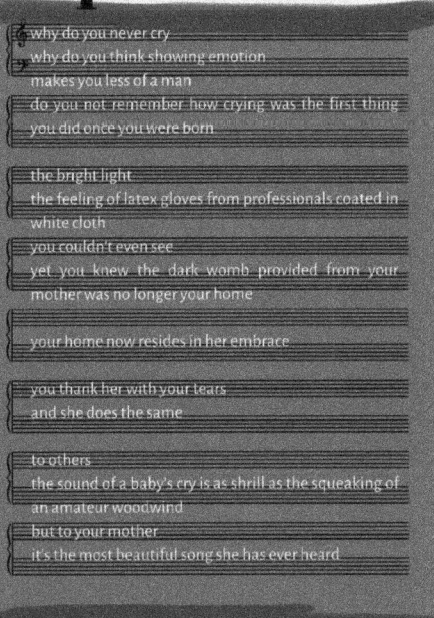

caleb sellers

prelude

why do you never cry
why do you think showing emotion
makes you less of a man
do you not remember how crying was the first thing
you did once you were born

the bright light
the feeling of latex gloves from professionals coated in
white cloth
you couldn't even see
yet you knew the dark womb provided from your
mother was no longer your home

your home now resides in her embrace

you thank her with your tears
and she does the same

to others
the sound of a baby's cry is as shrill as the squeaking of
an amateur woodwind
but to your mother
it's the most beautiful song she has ever heard

3

"The Gift . . ." connects with a later poem to reflect the evolution of parenting across generations.

the gift...

Women, what beautiful beings of great power
to have the gift of creating of life makes you closer to God knowing you are
also the Creator

to be the first of boys in your family
having only older sisters and a mother in your home makes you understand
the instinctive power of taking care of those you love

a man in a man's world born to be a mama's boy

you love your mother more than yourself
and a sister is simply a reminder of the life your mother had before you

as a man you will inherit the gift
the gift of taking care of those you love
what was thought to be a woman's job
you will carry

in time...

4

I formatted the title to physically draw the reader's eyes
upward, mirroring the poem's gesture of looking up.

p
u
g
n
i
k
o
o
l

caleb sellers

you're now beginning to learn your role

with younger brothers
you see your purpose as another man in their life to look up to

fishing, hunting, playing outside, advice..
you taught them everything they needed to know

with respect and your head up high
you lead by example for what a man should be
you are the strongest tree near Bruce Creek
unable to flinch from the slightest gust of wind
stretching to the sky along with your expectations of yourself

your brothers are looking up
but so are you

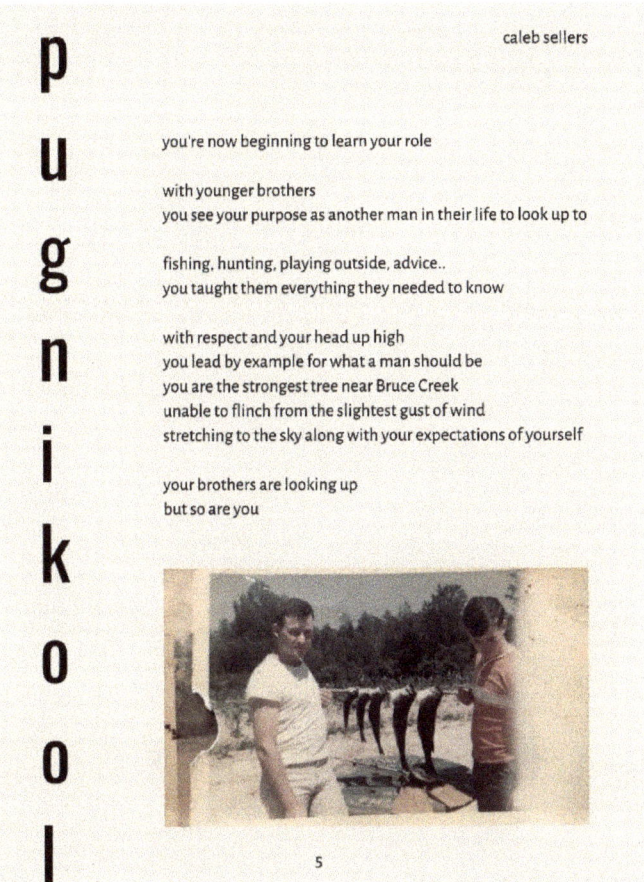

5

The italicized line is Cleve Earl's senior quote from his graduation at Walton High School.

in his image

man, both male and female: a miraculous creation in God's image
from dirt, dust, and clay we form into our vessels from just a breath of life
what glorious gifts He bestowed upon us

eyes, to see beyond ourselves and follow our destined path

the heart, to love everyone unconditionally

the mind, God's most complex creation that still cannot be explained
to think, translate many languages, discern the minds of others, and to never
stop working, shows how persistence always lives inside us

the mouth, a constant test of knowing your limits
God gave the mouth to his children to teach them lessons
at even their most vulnerable times
He gives them complete freedom in speaking whatever the mind strikes first
but the test is understanding that the mouth is not to be used at all times
what would that make God if he wanted his children to be able to speak ill of
Him and their siblings in Christ

after all

it is better to be silent and be thought a fool,
than to open your mouth and remove all doubt

6

20

Chapter II – Growin' Pains
a play on the television show

growin'
pains

Bill (Cleve Earl) fishing in his young adult years

I purposefully broke the first word in the title
to highlight the theme of breaking tradition
while also revealing the royalty we carry as children of God.

caleb sellers

brea-king tradition

blessed and highly favored
you were born to do great things in this world

since birth you have defied your family's expectations
and you have shown them countless times how God has blessed you

your journey is harder but greater than those that brought you into this
world

those that love you see greatness that cannot be explained

those that raised you see greatness that they never knew could from this
family

you are nothing but surprises

you received a greater education and sought to live your life with risks and
ever-evolving changes to become the greatest version of yourself

your wisdom is something that cannot be replicated
your soul and your past lives have given you the knowledge bestowed from
your creator
and to be in tune with that side of yourself is a treasure you found most are
still searching for

you are breaking tradition
but you've only left a crack
9

The picture was Cleve Earl's senior portrait,
and the font of the title shared its name. I remember
hearing a man say he was about to cry when he read this.

GRADUATE

dear pawpaw,

i'm writing to let you know that i am graduating from FSU with my bachelors this april

to both be the first ones in our family to graduate, you from high school, and me from college, i can honestly say that the more time passes, the more i see myself in you

thank you for giving me your gift of writing that summer night two years ago
it has taken me so far

you always wanted me to
write a book about you, so i did

this book has been therapy for me in more ways than one, and i am so excited to share it with everyone because i know that's what you want

this is my way of ending my bachelors degree by honoring the man that believed in my abilities the most

i love u, i miss u, and i thank u,
frog/pete

10

This photo was found in an old, Korean photo book
that my grandfather shared with his girlfriend
during his service in Korea. I wanted the title to honor that.

caleb sellers

한국

you served our country and you
served it well
with high ranking status
you lead a platoon and received an
honorable discharge

you were born to be a leader

i wished i asked more questions
because you lived an entire life before
meeting your wife and having
children and grand children and great
grand children

i believe in those years you found
yourself
and i am proud to say that i have done
the same thing

it took time away from home for us to
find our purpose
because in the end
it's the only thing that keeps us
yearning to do more and to never stop

our purpose is what fuels us to follow
our path
we did not create the path, but we
follow it with blindly

11

25

This prayer speaks with the spirit of
"Now I Lay Me Down to Sleep"—a lullaby told to me
by *my* mama—Cleve's daughter. This is her favorite poem.

lessons from valley view

a

mama's

prayer

bountiful love in a hug so tight
makes you feel safe in the depths of night
one tear that falls in the darkest of days
will be wiped off from her cause she loves you always
a worrisome problem that comes with great fear
is truly no match for Mom's bright spear
she is the woman that takes care of you
that one that stepped back to watch your dreams come true
thank her for selflessly showing the way
with bountiful love and wonderous praise
pray for your mother for she is one person
unable to carry everyone's burdens
help her out and show her your love
by being an example of her fathers above
because moms arent forever
and you'll find out some day
so cherish her blessings and love her always

12

Dale Dianne Paulk

Cleve bought this Camaro while he was back home after being honorably discharged. When I found this photo, I knew it had to be the centerfold—and back cover.

lessons from valley view

Why is the Camaro the pace car again?

Camaro has been named the Official Pace Car in the Indianapolis 500 for the second time in three years— a 50-year record! If you haven't driven the Hugger, take a hint from the guys at Indy. Maybe they know something you don't.

Camaro SS has what it takes. Again this year, it'll lead the pack at Indy.

Engine choices start with a 300-hp 350-cu.-in. V8 and run up through a 325-hp 396-cu.-in. job. There's even a new hood you can order with a super scoop intake that opens on acceleration, ramming cooler air into the engine for more power.

Mawmaw told me she first saw Pawpaw
driving this Camaro down the road where she lived
and that's how our family tree began: a 1969 Chevrolet

caleb sellers

Chevrolet Camaro

EARL

Because it's *the Hugger.*

Mr. and Mrs. Rushing

Chapter III – Full House
another play on a television show my mom loved

Daddy, Mama, Muffin, and Puddin

This poem is a continuation of "The Gift . . ."
Cleve had never took care of an infant until I was born.
He told Mawmaw it was one the best times of his life.

caleb sellers

...that keeps on giving

after all these years
including the ones with your new wife
you now welcome the life of two beautiful girls

they help you understand your mother's story
through the eyes of your daughters
as their father

times were different and you were tough
but you did your best with what you could
your patience was tested
and your wife did all of the caring
so your time to give the gift is not yet

fatherhood was a challenge
but it never stopped you from loving your daughters

you were given a second chance years later
when you were awarded the highest rank
"PAWPAW"

19

This title is from a picture frame of my cousins,
my sister, and me that rests by our grandparents' fireplace.

lessons from valley view

the blessing that is grandkids
this is your second chance
for the years missed out on not raising your daughters
you can repay them by raising their children

by showering your grandkids with love and quality time
you are showing your children that
you would do anything for their child if it meant helping you

you never talk about it
but you are so proud to see your children become better parents than you
thats what inspires you to be even better grandparents

with me
you were given a special second chance
with mama, dad, and mawmaw working
you were left to take care of me as a newborn
until they got off of work

this was the first time you had to take care of a child all by yourself
this is the gift
this opened a whole new world for you
you now know what it means to care for a child that you raised

my mother, your daughter, thanks you so much
she knows you love her now

20

This may not be a sentimental poem, but it captures the quiet, quality time I shared with my grandfather. I didn't always enjoy his hobbies—but I did them for him.

caleb sellers

How to Scale a Fish

step one
attempt at admiring your pawpaw's catch of the day

step two
beg your mawmaw not to scale fish with your pawpaw

step three
go scale fish with your pawpaw

step four
touch the catfish belly because it feels funny

step five
watch pawpaw skin a catfish in record breaking time

step four
grab the brim and glide the scaler towards the head until all the scales are off
then do it 50 more times

step five
go back inside and take a shower because that was gross

step six
realize you actually enjoyed scaling fish with pawpaw

21

I will never forget how small I felt looking up at the towering azalea bushes. Now, I see that's exactly how I looked up to Pawpaw—but I never felt small.

lessons from valley view

azaleas

my childhood is azaleas
the giant bushes in the front yard
so young and full of laughter

from jumping on your bed to the lion king song
to jumping on the trampoline
as you film every second so you never forget it

fishing and hunting
even when i didn't want to

listening to the songs you wrote
even when i didn't want to

helping you garden
even when i didn't want to

playing you my music
showing you my drawings
sharing you my essays

all the nicknames for every one of your children
puddin, muffin, doodle, fat boy, pete/frog, monkey, lil man

we are the azaleas and you are the bush

22

Chapter IV – Transition
Originally titled to match the poem.

My mom took this photo in the last few months we had with Pawpaw. It was later used as the portrait for his obituary. I think it's the best picture ever taken of him.

My mom helped me see Pawpaw's passing in a positive, celebratory light. She calls his funeral "his ceremony," and when we speak of death, we say, "he transitioned."

caleb sellers

transition

from another school day
to a drive back home

you did not die
you did not pass
you transitioned

mama says you never left
that you are always around

she sees the best in the family
when everyone else can't

there is no loss
because you are present elsewhere

you are here as i am writing this poem
you are in mama's dreams
you are in mawmaw's heart
you are alive in every memory replayed in our mind

we may still be in your house
but you are on your way home

25

The picture is the first house Cleve and Dianne bought after living with his mother, Mattie Rushing, for a time. I used to explore it with my cousins Chelsea and Chase.

lessons from valley view

you waved to mama through her kitchen window
and let her know that you were on your way to heaven

i knew why even after two years
you had not gone yet

you were waiting
waiting for mom to have her own place
and waiting for me to write your book

unfinished business now finished

you can rejoice now

you reside in your mother's embrace

welcome back home

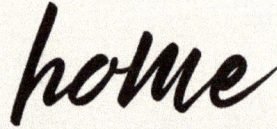

26

The title's font is reminiscent of the lettering on a dollar bill. Pawpaw used to gift me and my cousins "Frog money"—his special version of an allowance.

caleb sellers

grandfather / the patriarch / now our ancestor

you have lived so much life and yet so little
the life you have given your wife, your daughters, their daughters and sons, and
their sons and daughters will be cherished greatly

we thank you for the lessons you have taught us
the wisdom you have shared
and the advice you have told when even unsolicited

most times we did not listen
it took your disappearance to open our ears
except this time no one's talking

i wish you could come back to tell us your were right

the world needs your humility
your daughters need your brightness
your wife needs your presence
your grandchildren need your laughter
and your great-grandchildren need to know who you are

27

I mistakenly chose the wrong favorite flower to symbolize my grandmother. Although "Gardenias" concludes the collection better, I'm grateful this version came first.

magnolias

many tears have shed
and many days have passed

at first
there was a long drought
none of us could find peace in this family
everyone was hurt and no one knew how to handle the pain

i had never witnessed so much fighting
and all due to misdirected anguish

you really were the sun to this family
and no one knew it until now

many tears have shed
and many days have passed
but our tears have enriched our family roots
and we learned how to plant our new beginnings without you

it is mawmaw's time
she is our tree
and we are her magnolias

28

This caption was something I wrote for my Instagram post about Pawpaw's transition, and I felt deeply honored to share it with family and friends at his ceremony.

rest in peace pawpaw
not a day will go by where i won't think about you. you were the biggest inspiration to me and you will continue to be.

growing up, you taught me the importance of intelligence and self-respect through your 76 years of wisdom and experience. around this past year, i started to appreciate the time i shared with you because i never believed that i was too old to spend the night at your house the way i did when only you took care of me during my early years.
mawmaw told me two months ago, "pawpaw told me that the best times of his life was taking care of you." and that was the moment that made me realize how important my presence was in your life.

i always thought that because i never fish nor hunt you didn't see much in me, but you were the one that always saw potential in my writings, my academics, and my music because you had the same talents. for the only sibling to graduate form high school and make straight As and a man who let everyone know that you were the best at fishing and hunting (and you were), when i told you that i was getting my AA before graduating form high school you said "I couldn't do that." the only time you have ever said that in my lifetime, and it was about something your non-athletic, introvert, bookworm grandson did. i was bestowed the honor that you never gave to anyone else. so i will cherish these moments for the rest of my life knowing that some day we will sit in recliners and talk about how much i've accomplished since the last time you saw me. so until that day, take it easy, even though you never do.

With this project, I had never felt so deeply in my element, yet so wonderfully unfamiliar. Regardless, I knew this book was a gift of healing—for both myself and my family.

thank u

thank u caleb for learning how to create art through pain not only for ur
own therapy but for ur family's

pawpaw is proud and i love u
- caleb

This was the back cover. Honoring the purpose of this project: celebrating the life of Cleve Earl Rushing through the eyes of his grandson—Pete, Frog, Caleb.

2022

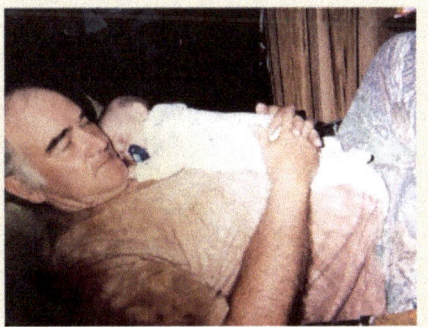

thank u, love u, miss u,
frog/pete

caleb sellers

intermission

PHOTO ALBUM

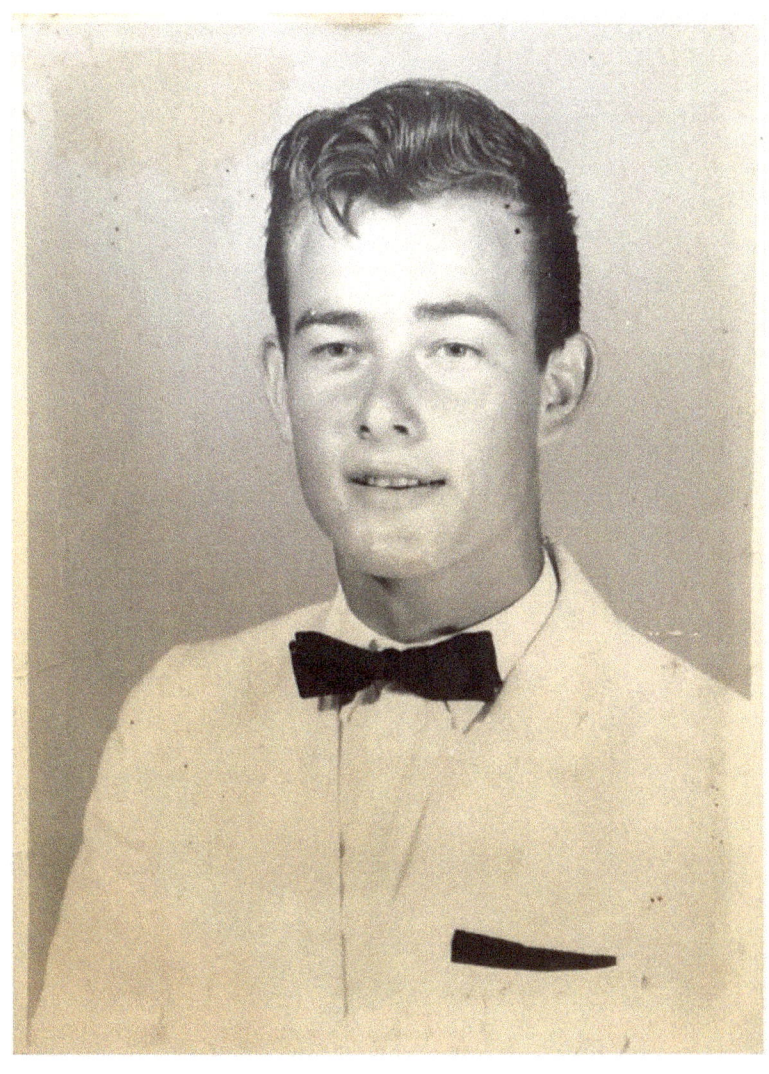

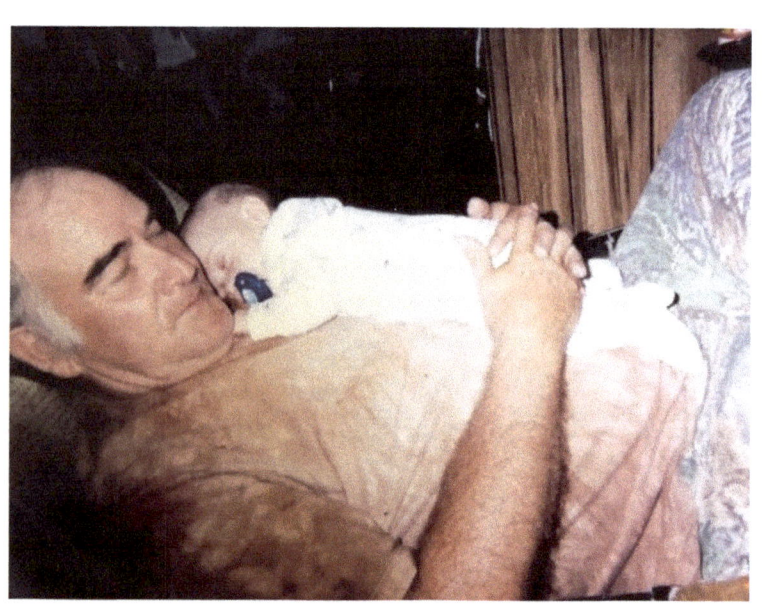

prelude ii

I have to say it now
It's been a good life and all
It's really fine
To have the chance to hang around
And lie there by the fire
While all my friends and my old lady
Sit and pass the pipe around

And talk of poems and prayers and promises
And things that we believe in
How sweet it is to love someone
How right it is to care
How long it's been since yesterday
What about tomorrow
What about our dreams
And all the memories we share

—   *John Denver, "Poems, Prayers and Promises"*

act ii

prologue

This poetry collection tells the story of my late grandfather, Cleve Earl Rushing, as I came to know him—through stories, memories, and the quiet lessons he passed down to us in Valley View, a hidden gem nestled between Ponce de Leon and DeFuniak Springs, Florida.

In writing this book, I've come to understand not only who he is, but how much of him lives in me.

These poems are written in remembrance and reflection—rooted in faith, family, and folklore.

These are *Lessons from Valley View.*

IN HIS IMAGE

Man

both male and female

a miraculous creation in His image

from dirt, dust, and clay

we are formed into our vessels

shaped by a single breath of life

what glorious gifts He has bestowed

Our eyes

to see beyond ourselves

to follow the path He set before us

Our heart

to love unconditionally

Our mind

God's most complex creation

still beyond explanation

to discern, translate, and think

to never cease its work

a testament to the persistence within us

Our mouth

a constant test of restraint

God gave His children voices

offering them the freedom to speak

whatever thought strikes first

but there is a lesson to be learned

It is better to be silent and be thought a fool

than to open your mouth and remove all doubt

PRELUDE

Why do you never cry
Why do you think showing emotion
makes you less of a man

Do you not remember
crying was the first time you ever sang

The bright light
the press of latex gloves
sterile and unfamiliar

You couldn't even see, yet you knew
the warmth of the womb was no longer home

You thanked her with your tears
she answered with her own

To many
a newborn's cry is shrill
like an amateur woodwind
but to your mother
it is the most beautiful song she has ever heard

Home is now your mother's embrace

THE GIFT

Women
what beautiful beings of great power
to carry the gift of creation is to stand nearer to God
knowing you, too, are the Creator

To be the first boy in a family of women
raised by a mother and older sisters
is to know the instinctive power
of nurturing those you love

A man in a man's world
born to be a mama's boy
You love your mother more than yourself
and a sister is simply a reminder
of the life she had before you

Though you are a man
you will inherit the gift
the gift of nurturing those you love

What once was thought a woman's work
you will carry in time . . .

LOOKING UP

You are learning your role
with younger brothers
you see your purpose
another man in their life to look up to

Fishing, hunting, running wild,

offering advice, speaking wisdom,

you taught them every lesson

they learned in Valley View

With respect, and your head held high

you lead by example

showing them what a man should be

You are the strongest tree

near Bruce Creek

unshaken by the wind

stretching toward the sky

where your own expectations of others reside

Your brothers are looking up

but so are you

BREAKING GENERATIONAL CYCLES

Blessed and highly favored

you were born to do great things

Since birth, you have defied expectations

proving countless times

that it is all because of Him

Your journey is harder

yet greater than those who came before you

those who love you see a brilliance

they will never understand

You pursued greater knowledge

embracing risks and constant change

reaching your fullest potential

Your wisdom is of God

inherited from your ancestors

to be in tune with that side of yourself

is a treasure most are still searching for

GRADUATE

I'm writing to let you know

that I have graduated from Florida State University,

and I now teach 12th Grade English

at my old high school. You would be so proud of me.

To both be the first ones in our family to graduate—

you from high school and me from college—

I can honestly say as the more time passes,

the more I see myself in you.

Thank you for passing your gift of writing to me

that summer night five years ago.

It has taken me so far.

You always wanted me to write a book about you,

so I did. I hope it's everything you wished for.

This book has been therapy for me in many ways,

and I am thrilled to share it with everyone.

I know that's what you'd want.

This is my way of honoring the man

that believed in me, and our gifts, the most.

I thank you. I miss you. I love you.

VETERAN

You served your country
and you served it well

I wish I could ask more questions
since you lived a life before us
your wisdom and knowledge
could help me understand
who I am
because of who I'm from

I believe in those years
you found yourself
and I am proud to say
that I have done the same

It took time away from home
for us to find our purpose
all to share it when we returned

Our purpose is what fuels us
to follow our path
and we do not plan it
but we move without question
for we were born to lead

A MAMA'S PRAYER

Bountiful love in a hug so tight
Makes you feel safe in the depths of night
Tears that fall on the darkest of days
Are wiped by her 'cause she'll love you always

A worrisome problem, that comes with great fear
Is truly no match for a mama's bright spir—
It warms her heart, she cares for you
So she paused her dreams for yours to come true

With bountiful love and fabulous praise
Thank her for selflessly showing the way
And pray for your mother, for she is one person
Unable to carry a pleth'ra of burdens

Give her your patience and show her your love
By being just like both her fathers above
'Cause moms aren't forever, you'll find out some day
So cherish your blessings and love her always

... THAT KEEPS ON GIVING

After all those years

including the ones with your wife

you welcomed the lives of two gorgeous girls

Your childhood home was reborn

built from the love of the women

who prepared you for this moment

Times were tough, and so were you

but you did your best with what you knew

You worked to exhaustion

crawling through the door

your youth left behind with the logs

Your wife carried the weight of nurturing

so the gift was yet to be given

It was a challenge

to be the best father

but that never stopped you

from loving your daughters

WONDER WOMAN

"Diana," he said

looking at his newborn

wise like trees

tough as nails

a Rushing nonetheless

Born from the craft

that was molded to her form

her power emits a shine

that others can only feel

I get why that's your name

you really are a wonder, woman

FATHER'S DAUGHTER

Born with the gift
to hold your Father's hand
dedicated to the obedience of the Lord
church was the home
that made you feel loved
when home itself could not

Faith intertwined

with the blood of the Valley

washes pure in the Holy Spirit

Bible verses memorized

to drown out the insults

child-like innocence

to cling to the life your younger self deserved

you pray yourself to sleep

in hopes that He will take care of you

You are much more than this life

You are my light

Now be theirs's

GRANDFATHER

Then life gave you a second chance
bestowing upon you
the greatest title of all

GRANDKIDS

A blessing

your second chance

For the years lost in raising your own

you repay them now

by raising theirs

By showering them with love

you show your children

that you will do anything for their child

if it means helping them

become the parent you never were

You may never say it

but you are so proud

to see them be better parents than yours

They inspire you

to be better than before

FROG

You were gifted with redemption

with Mama, Dad, and Mawmaw working

you were all that was left

to care for me

For the first time

you nurtured a child all on your own

The gift was given

HOW TO SCALE A FISH

Try to admire Pawpaw's catch of the day

Beg Mawmaw not to make you scale fish

Go scale fish with Pawpaw anyway

Touch the catfish belly because it feels funny

Watch Pawpaw skin the catfish
in record-breaking time

Grab the bream and glide the scaler toward its head
until all the scales are gone

Repeat fifty more times

Go inside and take a shower because that was gross

Eat the fish Mawmaw fried for dinner

Realize you enjoyed scaling fish with your Pawpaw

AZALEAS

My childhood is azaleas
the giant bushes in the front yard
so young, bursting with laughter

From jumping on your bed
to *The Lion King* song
to jumping on the trampoline
as you film every second
so you can relive each moment

Fishing and hunting
even when I didn't want to
gardening
even when I didn't want to
listening to your songs
even when I didn't want to

Playing you my instruments
showing you my drawings
reading you my essays
all because you wanted me to

NICKNAMES

Every bud
a nickname for a child

Puddin, Muffin,
Doodle, Fat Boy, Pete/Frog, Monkey,
Lil' Man

You are our bush
and we are your flowers

PAWPAW

Pawpaw, grandfather,
patriarch, ancestor
you have lived so much life
and yet so little

The life you have given your family
will be cherished greatly

We thank you for the lessons you have taught us
the wisdom you have shared
and the advice you have told
even when we never asked
I wish you'd come back to tell us you were right

The world needs your humility
your daughters need your brightness
your wife needs your presence
your grandchildren need your laughter
and your great-grandchildren
need to know who you are

It took your disappearance to open our ears
but this time no one's speaking

TRANSITION

From another day at school
to a quiet drive home
I brace myself
for the unexpected grief

You did not die
you did not pass
you simply transitioned

Mama says you never left
that you're always around
she sees the best in our family
when no one else can

There is no loss
for you are present elsewhere

You are in my purpose
you are in my mama's laugh
you're alive in every mem'ry
you are in my gifted craft

HOME

You waved to Mama
through her kitchen window
and let her know
you were on your way to Heaven

I knew why
even after two years
you had not gone yet

You were waiting
waiting for Mom
to have her own home
waiting for me
to write you your book

Unfinished business
now complete
and now so are you

You rejoice in your mother's embrace
welcome back home

GARDENIAS

There once was a drought
that dried our family roots
I witnessed so much pain
from grief that no one knew

No sun to our world
made us fall out of orbit
but a star burned so bright
that it beamed light like a rocket

He'll soar across his homeland
to bring his people back
and watch as every life he saves
be filled with love they lack

New life is brought to Earth
we heal from tortured pain
together we rejoice
in gardens of your name

Gardenias are the flowers
we now grow without you
nurtured from the lessons
you taught in Valley View

finale

AN ODE TO THE RUSHINGS

From gospel hymns rising between Oak Grove and Mt. Zion to the whistles echoing across Bruce Creek, music has always been our way of staying connected. I'll never forget the way Great Aunt Milbra made the harmonica sing, the local musicians who played their hearts out at the Valley View Community Center, or Pawpaw's many recordings of his favorite karaoke songs. Thank you for the gift of music.

From the portrait of Great Granny Mattie Rushing by Toma, to the sketches of Dickey Jones, to the high school art assignments Muffin once drew—creativity has always run through our veins. Thank you for the gift of artistry.

From lessons in how to fish, how to graph, how to cook, how to pray—to those taught in classrooms. Thank you for the gift of teaching.

From the creation of traps, boats, homes, and cars to the countless inventions that kept this family going for generations. Thank you for the gift of innovation.

Through the rewritten lyrics of his favorite songs, Pawpaw passed down more than just words—he gave me a way of seeing the world. I thank him for the gift of writing.

After hearing the beautiful stories about Pawpaw from Aunt Jeanie and Uncle Gary, I began to see more clearly how deeply he embodied all these gifts flowing through the Rushing bloodline. Beyond his many talents, it was his persistence, dedication, and faith that reminded me so much of the man I've become.

I feel born again in my appreciation and love for my grandfather. And with that renewal comes a deep respect and reverence for the many generations of Rushings who came before me. I never imagined that traditional American family values would bring me closer to God—but they have. And now, I carry profound pride in my heritage and the living presence of my ancestors in my life.

I am beyond blessed to come from a family whose generational gifts have shaped who I am. May you all find peace, love, and healing.

This book is for you.

curtain call

ACKNOWLEDGEMENTS

First and foremost, thank you, God, for blessing me with this beautiful, challenging, and rewarding life.

To Mama—thank you for your support and unwavering faith. You have taught me so much of what it means to be a true Christian that walks in the way of our Lord and Savior, Jesus Christ. I hope this book shows you the love I see your father had for you and how amazing of a mother you've always been.

To Dad—thank you for all the sacrifices you have made to make my life easier. You never deserved the pain you endured, but the wisdom and acceptance you have found is something so inspiring after all you have walked through. You are God's strongest soldier, and I pray to have an ounce of your resilience.

To Carly—thank you for always keeping me humble. You are capable of anything in this world, and I pray that you find success in a life fit for the princess you are.

To Gabriel—*there is no word that describes how I feel for you.* Your love and support inspire me daily to be the best version of myself, for myself. Thank you for believing in me. I cannot wait to spend the rest of my life with you. You are my angel.

To my best friends, Devyn, Donna, Isaiah, Chase, Logan, Bella, and Will—I love you all for everything.

You have all stuck by me since day one, and to see us all become so successful in each of our unique fields is a testimony to our limitless potential.

To my closest friends from home, John, Avery, Rachel, and Sam —thank you so much for your love and support. Your belief in my exceptionality reminds me why my story matters and why it must be shared. I love you all.

To the students of my hometown—thank you for inspiring me every day to fulfill a purpose that is much bigger than me. You have all given me so much love even at times when I felt undeserving. I will always love and support you.

To my cousins Chelsea and Chase—thank you for the memories. I know life has drifted us apart, but my admiration for each of you remains. This book is from us to him. I love y'all.

To Aunt Diana—thank you for being our family's Wonder Woman. You are the pillars of all pillars in this family, bringing us together with every holiday dinner, and supporting me in my journey as a teacher. Your support means the most to me, for I have always looked up to you and seen myself in you (the eldest).

To Mawmaw—I pray this book brings you healing in the parts of you that need it most. You deserve a life filled with joy and peace, and I hope to see you living in that feeling one day. I will always cherish your love.

director's notes

ABOUT THE AUTHOR

Caleb Clayton Sellers is a poet and artist rooted in the Florida Panhandle. Embracing the genre, Southern Gothic Romanticism, his work moves through themes of self-discovery, faith, and healing, shaped by his experiences as a gay Christian growing up in the rural South. With tenderness and honesty, Caleb shares his journey of reclaiming the parts of himself that he buried—inviting others to do the same.

Lessons from Valley View is the first release from his original self-publishing imprint, Rural Renaissance Publishing.

He is currently preparing to pursue his MA in English: Creative Writing at University of West Florida where he plans to create bodies of work from his rewritten roots.

You can connect with him on all social media platforms **@calebclaytonsellers**

encore

Eternity is a lifetime on Earth
but in Heaven it's only a day
my time with you was not long enough,
for I'm missing the light from your way

Your presence was warm like the sun on my skin
when four walls were no longer home
you always feel gone but I know you are here,
so I learn I'm never alone

Curses are breaking and roots will be tied
to make our family one
I bring them this gift, an offering of peace,
the war is finally won

I wish I had more time to say
the things I never did
I wish you knew how loved you were
since I was just a kid
you live through me for now I see
the man you've always been